Crossing The Night

by

Frances-Anne King

First published 2023 by The Hedgehog Poetry Press

Published in the UK by
The Hedgehog Poetry Press
5, Coppack House
Churchill Avenue
Clevedon
BS21 6QW

www.hedgehogpress.co.uk

ISBN: 978-1-913499-91-4

For Elena, Alice, Sebastian and William

'A fidelity to the ungraspable lies in the very root of both biological existence and what we experience in beauty.'

Jane Hirshfield
(Hiddenness, Uncertainty, Surprise)

Contents

MEDITATION

11 pm and still light.
A glow of amber
behind a trail of charcoal cloud

shaped like a brachiosaurus
loping the sky's vast plain
in search of prey.

This is the hour
when tidy knots of certainty
loosen and fall away,

let you dip into your shadows,
write yourself across
the forgiving page of night.

SOME SAY THAT TO DREAM OF FLYING IS A SIGN OF HAPPINESS

After 'Vesper Flights' by Claire Macdonald

Up she floats
calm as a helium balloon
past a sheen of plate glass windows
steel-gleam   fingers of light probing a dusk

alive with the dream-flutter of   nectuid moths
tiny spiders hoisted on strands of charged silk
aphids   lacewings
                    the high cry of bats

oh she is fluid in her lightness
so porous   all creatures of windborne migration
flow through her   their drift a pulse in her blood
                                        a heartbeat

lofted higher
            a glass-topped forest of skyscrapers
                                shimmers below

she is all feathers now
the white-flagged wings of nighthawks
the arrowed peregrine lunging for prey
the wheeling vesper flight of swifts rising
                                through cloud
to calibrate their compasses

she is wing-beat   urgency
drawn towards the unseen
just out of reach in a grey cloud-mass
that opens   whitens   blurs   fades
                            and she is falling

slowly falling   into the drag of gravity
reeled in   to the dawn of another day
                            her body

CROSSING THE NIGHT

After 'The Jetty' by Alastair Magnaldo

We will cross into unmapped territory,
(the journey was arranged many years ago)
walk down the ancient jetty, it's wood
worn thin, silvered and brittled
                              by innumerable footfalls.

Soon a boat will carry us across the slate blue
rippled sea where no wind blows. We have packed
hope in our suitcases, strains of music, songs,
something whispered long ago,
                              children's laughter.

There are few of us here, though we know
millions have crossed over before us
and countless will follow.
(This is not so much a place
                              as a sense of transition.)

Love is too precious to be packed; we cling
to its thread, feel its constant tug.
We each hold a vision. Mine is a house
by the Agean, a tall cedar and Venus
                              always rising.

DREAM IN MEXICO CITY

Watch where you walk, said the guide,
the forest floor is dangerous

so I stepped off the high pavement
onto an empty boulevard

where huge, potted jacarandas
swayed with the weight of hummingbirds

whose song was red, green, orange, blue –
fine tendrils of sound that twined round

and round my body and my guide
said, *Now you meet Montezuma* .

WAKING

There are those dreams that trail behind you
days after you've dreamt them, when half awake,
you're still pulled down by a magnet or current –

like the night you dream a three-act opera in a language
you know but don't know, are left aching with something
like Cio-Cio San's last parting.

Or that other dream, where the pale-skinned boy
shines with such dreadful beauty he scorches your mind,
leaves you wounded for days.

WOODPECKER

No shy visitation hopping across my lawn this year.
It felt like a month had been lost from the calendar –

something necessary erased, leaving a shift of unease,
like when you see banks of lavender without the bees.

And then today, watching the way light thieved its way
through leaves of the old apple tree, playing the shade

with tiny iridescences – a streak of black and white,
the quick sure movement of a hammer head striking

the bark again and again and that flash of scarlet
that made me think of Turner's last minute buoy –

the way it anchored his painting
                        to something beyond itself.

HOME THOUGHTS FROM THE RED PLANET

It was considered weakness to look back
so they didn't speak of it, but images
spored inside their heads and spread
across their dreams at night. Some stashed
files, chose rare fonts – as if to keep the past
alive more vividly. Some wrote of trees;
oak, aspen, cypress, silver birch, pelts
of balsam fir across a mountain range,
the shape and texture of a leaf, the vibrancy
or calm of some particular shade of green.

A man described a wheat field ripening under sun,
the weight and sea-sway of wind-pulled crops.
A woman, haunted by cycles of return, explained
the pattern play of swallows in an autumn sky;
how they forage on the wing, the skim and swoop
of cobalt feathers across the surface of a lake.
Another recorded the last bee she'd seen, a red carder,
and sketched it in the margins of each page.
Through all their notes the memory of blue
in all its myriad shades, repeated and repeated.

PLACE OF ARCHES

Oaxaca, Mexico

repeats
like a note of music,
or a bird call's soft insistence
through the heat of summer
behind the children's laughter

a place
where sunlight filters
onto worn flagstones
as if decanted from an ancient stillness
that has smothered the stutter
of machine guns, splintering glass,
the muffled wails of mothers

a place
where curves carve something
of infinity across the mind –
an enduring grace
that never breaks its silence

MOSQUE AT CORDOBA

A receding murmur through the infinity of arches
as the guided group diminish in the distance, demonstrating

yet again the architect's intention to show
the inconsequence of our existence. Their footsteps tap –

stilettos, sandals, flip flops, trainers – on worn flagstones,
disturbing nothing more than sleeping dust.

For a moment, alone in the palm of stillness, I look up,
see the horse-shoe arch at the entrance to the Mihrab –

its perfect symmetry shaping my mind to something other.
The veil is thin here. Ghost prayers, centuries old, rise

to the framing of gold tesserae – a dazzling mosaic of countless
minute pieces, creating a grace of calligraphy,

flowers and leaves Eve might have picked in her earthly paradise.
Here the indefinable is sought through perfect geometry

and earth's abundance. If stones could mourn, these would call
for the living prayer denied them.

I conjure a land where the oak and the pomegranate intertwine,
where the sparrow and the bulbul nest together.

PEMBROKESHIRE QUILT

1915

After the telegram arrived
she rolled out satin cotton,
took softest lambs-wool wadding –
recalling mountain rambles,
how they picked fleece from crevices
in stone walls, hedges, ditches,
how she taught him to card wool
to remove twigs and thistles.
Sunlight sparked her rows of threaded needles
in their scarlet velvet cushion
turning them to minute bayonets and lances.
She didn't need her templates,
the tailor's chalk moved smoothly
as if her hand had somehow
always known this journey.
A starfish medallion, two borders,
one of waves and shells,
one of flowers and fern fronds,
then acorns in each corner. Stars and spirals –
so many spirals, as if this emblem of eternity
might reel him in a fraction closer –
the child whose kingdom was an oak wood,
who came home at dusk
the smell of green a song on him;
the beachcomber who collected ammonites,
egret's feathers, salt-washed wood
buffed smooth as bone in moonlight;
the boy who learned the constellations,
told her the stars' white shining
was already in the past.

When finished the quilt was folded,
taken up the mountain to that place
where stone cromlechs covered
ancient warriors, where fields
and wooded valleys sloped down
to a gentian sea. Here she buried it –
in earth his bones would never rest in.

LIE OF SHADOW 1

On a wall in Tate St Ives there's a small oil painting of an
empty Elizabethan room, its wainscoted walls dappled with
radiance flowing in from a mullioned window, which must
look out on water, because the quality of light demands it.
There's an open book on the table, a page lifted by a breeze,
a lute propped against a chair, and you know with absolute
certainty that someone has just left the room although there's
nothing to point to this conclusion.

SPARROWS

Only sparrows broke the two minute silence,
their chorus of chatter loud, insistent,
ricocheting from building to building
as the sun ran truant over polished leather,
sword hilts, medals, the bell of a trombone;
and I wondered – in the early days
of the Great War, before green was blasted
and ground shelled into a bloody quagmire
if the song of sparrows was the last sound
soldiers heard in the lull before the whistle blew.

SONS

1940, 1945, 1946

I breathed their history like air –
careless of it, riding my youth high.
But now their pictures steal
from family albums, slip
into the shadow of my sons –
like silent sentinels, gaining substance
from a mouth, a cheekbone,
the fall of hair across a brow.
They merge with living flesh
crowding my light with quiet haunting.

How did their mother live her dust of days?

AFTER THE ROMANS LEFT

A room suffused with amber light.
An elderly couple, their evening meal
spread out across a table: a low table
laden with dormice dipped in honey,
pheasant, dark olives,
harvested walnuts and the last flask
of their Roman wine.

Dialogue seeps soft and slow
as if rising through deep water.
They wonder who will tend the vines
now old Sirius is dead.
Shortages are touched on briefly:
pepper running low,
no cinnamon to spice the apple cake.

When a neighbour stumbles in
with news of sightings:
ships in the estuary
dark smoke on the horizon,
painted people crossing the wall
and moving southwards,
the couple speak in coded calmness.

Too old to leave with Maximus,
they have buried their gold and silver
in the woods. Their treasure
will lie untouched for centuries.
Amber light sinks to shadow. Dark
spins down like ashes. Hand in hand
they walk into the almost-night.

VOLUBILIS

You must time it right –
which is all down to luck –
hope the shepherd has chosen that moment
to usher his flock of long-eared sheep
and rangy goats across the narrow road,
so the coach load of tourists,
armed to the hilt with video cameras
have to wait on agrarian time.

Then the ruins can unfold,
arrange themselves – show you the ruts
of chariot wheels in stone, slant light
in such a way that Orpheus's scops owl
pipes from his mosaic branch
as a stream of ghosts circle and pass through you –
intent on buying fresh fish, savouring
new wines, comparing the liquid gold
of their olive oil, their gaze
momentarily transfixed
by a pair of storks building a ramshackle nest
on the roof of a house where today
another pair perch on a solitary pillar
at the entrance to a basilica –
open now to the same wide-eyed sky
that blessed their fertile plain with light,
touched these wild marigolds with flame.

POSTCARD 1

Just to say, today the sea was the colour
of a mackerel's belly with that particular
stillness of an always moving thing
and as the sun set behind a cloud line
its contours flared with a filament of white
and then the sky bled

BARREL JELLYFISH

I find you at the tide mark –
where salt-smoothed twigs
scatter the sand like rune-sticks –
stripped of all water-grace,
jumbled and clumsy,
your huge dome dimly revealing
funnels, cogs and wheels
all stilled to ghost shades.
The scalloped edge of your umbrella
scored with an indigo line
like an ancient warrior's woad tattoo –
and those coral pink stinging tentacles,
wantonly splayed across the sand,
glisten in death
with an alien decadence.
Strange survivor –
no heart, no bones, no brain –
floating down millennia,
I wonder will your kind be here
when mine has gone,
replaced by brains
ten thousand times the speed of man's?

POSTCARD 2

not much to say today except my fingertips
are raw from scrabbling at the rough rim
of the world, trying to stop it from tipping

PANIC

Off the grid,
somewhere in my head
there's a field
where a vermillion queen
has brought her swarm
to form a hive;
tiny scarlet creatures
executing orders,
dancing a mosaic,
searching out the fear-flower,
the hidden apprehension-blossom,
and the deep throated
violet bloom
of anticipated loss.
Why *my* head, I ask her,
aren't there richer pastures
to be plundered?
But there's never a reply,
she just lies in the hub
of her multi-chambered mansion
growing bloated on my loss.
It seems I can't evict her,
though sometimes she's restless,
wants to try a new location,
sends a drum roll down my arteries,
leads her swarm into my throat
then spearheads her army
to the chambers of my heart
in a frenzied tachycardia.

NOTES FROM BEDLAM

I am paper. Fingers flame with scarlet fire.
I am bone china. The hammer of words will shatter me.
I have woven cobwebs round my body. Eyes throw thorns, long as lances.

Thoughts fold into books I never read and put on the top shelf.
I see the oak tree outside my window, count the leaves on a single branch,
then count them again. Trees breathe calm. They live in the now.
I pick pebbles on the beach. Each is a memory I drown in the sea.

The raven's wing spills soot. It will choke me.
The rasp of spreading feathers deafens me.
Even the tiny wren: see how its quills shine tips of steel
to razor through my flesh.

I am deconstructing; the bones of my skull have burst apart
my eyes have slipped through the open window,
my arms left me in the night, my legs melt like warm butter.
Now I am a stone rolling through the door.

THE SKULL COLLECTORS

A mind can be calmed
by the balm of numbers,
soothed by their beauty
of precision, the absolute,
the non negotiable.
Think how the symmetry
of Fibonacci prevents
a crack from which a sliver
of speculation might spill out.
Imagine heads stripped
of flesh, muscle, brain, soaked
in limewater to whiten
bone to shell-like purity,
as if the gleam of crania –
their smooth contours – could
capture the essence of
a being by measurements
with craniophores,
anthropometers, spreading
and sliding callipers –
hundreds of instruments
specific to a head:
the density of bone,
the shape and volume
of a brain, eye sockets,
zygomatic arches,
protuberances and apertures,
all noted and filed
in Thesaurus Craniorum –
a phalanx of figures
waiting for resurrection.

HEART

Each night she lies in bed,
listens to her heart's percussive
knocking from basement to attic,
sometimes a scratch, a thud,
a ceaseless pecking,
as if an animal menagerie
of wild, exotic creatures
is in residence.

Sometimes a line from a song
drifts the dark, coils
like a smoke-ring around her;
a stray scent - musk roses, oranges,
the mineral smell of blood.
How can she live with this heart
holding such freight,
wearing its old walls thin.

BALNAKEIL

Do you remember that exhibition,
a microscope laid out for us to inspect,

the smear of sand across the slide that changed
under the lens to multicoloured particles of

stone, glass, rock, shell, every one different,
and how despite their journey through millennia

battered and ground by seas, they still survive
to illustrate geology. A huge expanse of pale,

fine sand stretches out behind us as we stand here
at the water's edge. We leave our footprints

with those of oyster catchers, black headed gulls
and arctic terns. Whatever we choose to give

of ourselves to the sand it takes and disperses
to the wind's will or the wash of a cleansing tide.

NAUTILUS

after 'Nautilus' Michael Eden, 2015

Sunbeams flood
its fretwork with the force

of water,
as if to melt its solidity –

perhaps
allow its liquid form

to uncurl at night,
        float

sodium-lit streets,
trawling for that rich, thick

juice of dreams
that pulse through shadows.

It could be
a pelagic mollusc

reinvented as a helmet
Achilles might have worn –

a present
from his sea nymph mother –
or,

the skull of some
extra- terrestrial invader,

discovered in the burning sands
of Arizona.

A real nautilus
          swims deep,
resists great pressure;

as it grows it seals its past off
               chamber by chamber –
never revisits it.

Lucky nautilus – or is it? –
living in the water's moment,

unable to regret,
to hear the mind's faint knocking,

its whispered words
or that creak of movement
          behind a frail partition.

It just
moves forward into larger spaces,

slowly increasing
its almost perfect spiral;

carries
nothing but its own creation,

adapts
to different waters

as it drifts those
          deep, dark slopes

of stricken coral reefs,
unfazed by fading light.

If
I could run my fingers

across this glassed-off sculpture,
roam its scrollwork

for a moment,
swim like the nautilus,
                    innocent of need...

POSTCARD 3

all night
I walked my mind-fields
corralling stars
inside a fence of hope

INFINITE POSSIBILITY

When I walked into that night –
hoar-frost cold, every star in the sky
there for the picking,

an east wind cut my moorings,
set me spinning in sparked air
like a seed pod, up and up

till the world was a speck
and constellations hummed
like a hive of summer bees

and the dark split open then,
pomegranate ripe, spilling more light
than one lifetime could hold.

OCEAN

Swim down

to curtains of bright shadow
        to threads of light
woven through the water

swim deeper

to where rainbows reduce
        red fades
leaves twilight
        silver grey
with opalescent creatures

deeper

light turns misty
        green dims
blue blooms
        cold and brilliant

deeper

curling opaque strands
        reach down
to almost darkness

a place

        of bleached bones
a ghost of starlight
        where sea-life flashes
bioluminescent

pale octopus
        amphipod
glassy arpeggios
        of leg, tail, antenna
trailing
        primeval silence

THE TIME YOU ARE NO LONGER PART OF

Forgive this weakness but I need to place you somewhere –
perhaps you spin inside a brilliant constellation?

How many million light years might you have passed through?
I try, but just can't hold this concept in my head.

Did you leave all your memories here on Earth
or do you still sense your garden; the drift of cherry blossom,

the vagrant scent of night stock, Turk's-cap lilies,
those banks of lavender alive with bees?

Let me set you in Messier 81, its arms spiralling and vast,
full of interstellar dust, regions of fluorescent gas

and blinding stars between those luminous greens, reds, blues.
On certain nights when Ursa Major's clarity

lasers through my head, time becomes a kite string
straining to break free into the wind.

CHILD

I hear him call her *little bear*
and think of Ursa Minor –
of how the North Star
                           anchors it
yet gives it slack
enough to write a path
of time and light
                      across the sky.

FOOTNOTES

Page 24   Volubilis: The partly excavated Berber city in Morocco, thought to be the ancient capital of Mauretania.

Page 29   Notes from Bedlam. *After: 'Bedlam. The asylum and beyond' Exhibition at The Wellcome Collection 2016*

Page 30   The Skull Collectors: On the death of the craniometerist Joseph Barnard Davies one obituary noted 'his strong points were untiring energy in the collection and record of specimens rather than any deep power of observation, judgement or induction.'

ACKNOWLEDGEMENTS

Acknowledgements are due to the editors of the following magazines, in which many of these poems, or versions of them, first appeared: *Acumen, Agenda, Interpreter's House, The Littoral Press, Poetry Salzburg Review, Scintilla, The High Window,* and *Raceme.* 'Son's' was published in *The Leaf Books* Poetry Anthology 2006, (with the University of Glamorgan). 'Heart' won 3rd prize in *The Interpreter's House* poetry competition in 2017 and 'Child' was highly commended. 'Home Thoughts from the Red Planet won 1st Prize in the 2018 *St Hilda's and the Poet's House Oxford,* Science and Poetry Competition and is published in the winners pamphlet, *Haunted by Cycles of Return,* Poems about Climate Change 2019.

My sincere thanks to members of the *Subversifs* and *Clock-House* poetry groups for their insight and advice on earlier drafts. Huge thanks to highly talented artist, David Humphries, for allowing me to use his painting as my cover image.